The Peace Bible

THE PEACE BIBLE
Words from the Great Traditions

with a foreword by
Hans Küng

Compiled and edited by
Steven Scholl

KALIMÁT PRESS
LOS ANGELES

Library of Congress Cataloging in Publication Data

The Peace Bible.

1. Peace—Religious aspects. 2. Sacred books.
I. Scholl, Steven, 1954–   .
BL65.P4P43 1986   291.1'7873   86–15169
ISBN 0-933770-50-2

Kalimát Press
1600 Sawtelle Boulevard, Suite 34
Los Angeles, California 90025

(Continued on page 117)

CONTENTS

FOREWORD
by Hans Küng

All religions teach peace, although they have also condoned and even glorified war. This evident historical reality demands that we ask: What today should form the basis of our attitudes toward the world religions? Instead of an indifferentism which finds everything equally valid: more indifference toward those orthodoxies that make themselves the full measure of salvation, or lack of salvation, for human beings and seek to establish the truth of their claims with instruments of power and force. Instead of a relativism which rejects all absolutes: more sensitivity to the relativity of every human arrangement of absolutes which hinders a productive coexistence among various religions; and more sensitivity to the relationality which allows us to see every religion within its own web of relationships. Instead of a syncretism where everything—possible and impossible—is mixed together and melted into one: more commitment to a synthesis of points of opposition between religions, so that instead of war, hate, and dispute which still take their daily toll in blood and tears, *peace* may reign among the religions.

In the face of religious impatience, we cannot ask for too much patience, *religious freedom.* There must be no betrayal of freedom for the sake of truth. But at the same time, there should be no betrayal of truth for the sake of freedom. The question of truth must not be trivialized and sacrificed to the utopia of a future world unity and one world religion. On the contrary, we are all challenged to think through anew, in an atmosphere of freedom, the whole question of truth. For freedom, other than arbitrariness, is not simply freedom from all obligations and bindings —that is purely negative. Rather, it is at the same time a positive freedom requiring new responsibility toward one's fellow human beings, toward one's self, and toward the Absolute. True freedom, therefore, is a freedom for truth.

One could proceed here with long and complicated discussions on the question of what truth is and take a position on the various contemporary theories about truth (correspondence, reflection, consensus, and coherence theories). Yet the question of true religion must remain very much in the foreground. As a presupposition for everything that follows concerning the lack of truth in religion, I offer this thesis as a starting point: The Christian possesses no monopoly on truth, and also no obligation to forego a confession of truth on the grounds of an arbitrary pluralism. Dialogue and witness do not exclude each other. A confession of the truth includes the courage to sift out untruth and speak about it.

It would certainly be a gross prejudice to identify ahead of time the border between truth and untruth as identical to the border between one's own and other religions. If we are serious, we must grant that the borders between truth and untruth run through each of our religions. So often we are both correct and incorrect! Criticism of another position, therefore, is made responsibly only on the basis of a decisive self-criticism. Likewise, only thus is an integration of the values of the other possible. That means that within religions not everything is equally true and good. There are also elements in religious teachings, in beliefs and customs, in religious rites and practices, within institutions and authorities that are not true and not good. This applies to Christianity, as well as to all other religions.

With the issue of peace, as with all other issues, it is appropriate that we focus our attention on those positive teachings in all faiths that conduce to the good of humanity.

PREFACE

The United Nations has proclaimed 1986, International Year of Peace. This act and the many other actions worldwide in support of peace, disarmament, and international cooperation are signs of hope in a time of crisis. The threat of nuclear war haunts humanity, while the superpowers espouse peace through nuclear terror (Mutually Assured Destruction) and continue unabated the madness of the arms race— even to the stars. Concurrently, conventional warfare, terrorism—largely sponsored and supplied by the same superpowers, starvation, and violations of human rights continue to plague the world community. In this time of pain, struggle, and hope, the world's religions are confronted with a test of faith.

This test is perennial, it is recorded in all scriptures. The Bible, Qur'an, Mahabharata, I Ching, and Bhagavad-Gita all are mixed bags of exhortations to peace and calls for holy war. Sadly, scripture has too often been used to promote war or to spread salvation through violence. Religious peacemakers must not only speak peace to the political powers who wage war, they must also speak peace to coreligionists who support, directly or indirectly, war and oppression. As Hans Küng observes in his foreword, the borders between truth and untruth pass through every faith.

War and peace and religion are inextricably bound together as existential human conditions of being-in-the-world. We are at war with the violent images that rise from our freelings of anger, hurt, rejection, and suffering. And we are at peace within loving relationships of family and community, in the solitude of prayer and meditation, or in communion with nature. The problem of war is a psychological problem as well as a political, social, and economic problem. The world's religions recognize that the problem of war is related to these conditions as well as to matters of faith and spirituality.

For people of faith, the world is the arena where we must struggle to attain peace. Not merely the absence of war, but peace as the experience of wholeness, love, and harmony: with ourselves, with other persons, with the natural world, and with God. In its best moments, religion has called out for peace within a warring world and demanded that just and equitable relationships be established among alienated factions of society. Historians of religion have long noted that great religious figures, Moses, Amos, Jeremiah, the Buddha, Jesus, Muhammad, Bahá'u'lláh, all preached against the political order of their day. The religious critique is in need of constant renewal, otherwise religion becomes a barrier to liberation and salvation, becoming identified with power and privilege in this world. Communities of faith are obligated by their belief in a loving God of Justice and Mercy to stand against any worldly power that threatens the peace and well-being of individuals or community.

Religion, then, must meddle in the affairs of the world. God commanded Moses to argue and dispute with Pharaoh; Jesus overturned the tables of the moneylenders; and Muhammad founded a state. Today, religious communities continue to arise and speak out for justice and peace. Buddhists, Jews, Christians, Muslims, Hindus, Bahá'ís, and others are meeting the crisis of our time by mobilizing their communities and joining together in a grassroots effort to shift the weight of history from war to peace.

The activities of the world's religions for peace are impressive. They continue to escalate. International ecumenical peace groups, such as the World Conference of Religions for Peace and the International Fellowship of Reconciliation, provide forums for members of the world's religions to meet, share insights, and plan courses of action. In America, Europe, Latin America, India, and Asia, the religious community has become a mainstay of national peace movements.

The strengths that religion brings to the peace movement are many. Religion takes a value-based approach to social and political issues—beginning with prayerful reflection on themes of the sanctity of life; the value of community; the nature of evil; the dignity of the individual; preference for the poor, the stranger, or the minority; and the need for reciprocity and love in our dealings with others. Religion testifies to the power of love and to the mystery of the Holy in human life. As demonstrated through the writings and lives of Gandhi and Martin Luther King, Jr., principles of nonviolence and noncooperation with evil have had a great impact on the peace movement in this century. This theory and praxis of nonviolence is grounded in scripture—not just biblical, but (especially in the case of Gandhi) in reflections on the Bhagavad-Gita, the Qur'an, and Buddhist texts as well.

The Peace Bible draws from the wisdom found within the religious traditions of humanity. The work is not comprehensive, but rather a modest compilation of scripture, with some commentary, on themes of peace and justice. We hope that it will make a small contribution to the ecumenical peace movement and to the emergence of that world-embracing vision so necessary in our time of crisis and hope.

STEVEN SCHOLL
LOS ANGELES

The Peace Bible

The Promise of Peace

The wolf shall dwell with the lamb, and the
   leopard shall lie down with the kid,
and the calf and the lion and the fatling
   together, and a little child shall lead them.
The cow and the bear shall feed;
   their young shall lie down together;
   and the lion shall eat straw like the ox.
The suckling child shall play over the hole of
   the asp, and the weaned child shall put his
   hand on the adder's den.
They shall not hurt or destroy in all my holy
   mountain;
for the earth shall be full of the knowledge of
   the Lord as the waters cover the sea.

JEWISH SCRIPTURES
The Book of Isaiah

To dwell in a peaceful land, with right desires
   in one's heart—
This is the greatest blessing.
Control of self and peaceful speech, and
   whatever word be well spoken—
This is the greatest blessing.
To live righteously, to give help to kindred, to
   follow a peaceful calling—
This is the greatest blessing.

BUDDHIST SCRIPTURES
Words of the Buddha

When the inevitable day has come,
And none shall doubt its coming:
Day that will abase! Day that will exalt!
When the earth shall be shaken,
And the mountains crumbled
Into dust.
And you all into three bands divided:
How happy shall be the people of the Right
   Hand!
How wretched the people of the Left Hand!
And those foremost in faith, foremost still!
These are they who will be nigh unto God,

In gardens of delight . . .
No vain discourse shall they hear therein, nor
    any falsehood,
But only the cry, "Peace! Peace!"

ISLAMIC SCRIPTURES
Qu'ran, Sura 56

Great is peace. At the hour
that the Messiah reveals himself to Israel, at that
hour the first word he speaks will be "Peace."

JEWISH TRADITION
The Talmud

May peace reign on earth.
May the gourd and the pot agree. May their
animals live in harmony and all evil words be
banished into the bush and the vacant forest.

AFRICAN TRADITIONS
A prayer from Guinea

The truest and greatest power is the strength of Peace . . . because Peace is the will of the Great Spirit.

NATIVE AMERICAN
Hopi Declaration of Peace

May wise submission conquer disobedience in this place, and may peace triumph over discord here, and generosity over greed, reverence over blasphemy, truthful speech over lying words. May the Righteous Order gain victory over the lie.

ZOROASTRIAN SCRIPTURES
The Yasna

For to us a child is born, to us a son is given; and the government will be upon his shoulder, and his name will be called "Wonderful Counselor, Mighty God, Everlasting Father, Prince of Peace."

Of the increase of his government and of peace there will be no end . . . with justice and with righteousness from this time forth and for evermore.

JEWISH SCRIPTURES
The Prophet Isaiah

That all nations should become one in faith and all men as brothers; that the bonds of affection and unity between the sons of men should be strengthened; that diversity of religions should cease, and differences of race be annulled—what harm is there in this? . . . Yet so it shall be; these fruitless strifes, these ruinous wars shall pass away, and the "Most Great Peace" shall come. . . . Do not you in Europe need this also? Is not this that which Christ foretold? . . . Yet do we see your kings and rulers lavishing their treasures more freely on means for the destruction of the human race than on that which would conduce to the happiness of man-

5

kind . . . These strifes and this bloodshed and discord must cease, and all men be as one kindred
and one family. . . . Let not a man glory in this,
that he loves his country; let him rather glory in
this, that he loves his kind.

BAHÁ'Í FAITH
Words of Bahá'u'lláh

In the *Lotus Sutra* chapter titled
"The Divine Power of the Tathāgata" we read:
"with various flowers, incense, garlands, cano-
pies, as well as personal ornaments, gems, and
wonderful things, they all from afar strewed the
sahā-world (world of suffering). The things so
strewn from every quarter were like gathering
clouds, transforming into a jeweled canopy, cover-
ing all the place above the buddhas."
. . . This is the "one buddha-land" of spiritual
life; and if spiritual life reaches this state, the
actual world cannot but change accordingly.
That is to say, a world of great harmony will
appear when all nations, all races, and all classes
come to love in accordance with the one truth, so

that discrimination among them vanishes, discord and fighting do not occur, and all the people work joyfully, enjoy their lives, and promote culture. In short, the whole world will become one buddha-land.

NIKKYO NIWANO
The Buddhist Approach to Peace, 1977

What in history has been called peace has never, in fact, been aught other than an anxious or an illusory blissful pause between wars. . . . May we, then, cherish the hope that the countenance which has remained unknown to all previous history will shine forth on our late generation, apparently sunk irretrievably in disaster? Are we not accustomed to describe the world situation in which we have lived since the end of the Second World War no longer even as peace but as the "cold" phase of a world war declared in permanence? In a situation which no longer even seeks to preserve the appearance of peace, is it not illusory enthusiasm to speak of the great peace which has never existed being within reach?

It is the depth of our crisis that allows us to hope in this way. Ours is not a historically familiar malady in the life of peoples which can eventuate in a comfortable recovery. Primal forces are now being summoned to take an active part in an unrepeatable decision between extinction and rebirth. War has not produced this crisis; it is, rather, the crisis of man which has brought forth the total war and the unreal peace which followed.

MARTIN BUBER (1878–1965)

The Evil of War

They came forward, seized Jesus, and held him. At that moment one of those with Jesus reached for his sword and drew it, and he struck the High Priest's servant and cut off his ear. But Jesus said to him, "Put away your sword. All who take up the sword shall die by the sword."

CHRISTIAN SCRIPTURES
The Gospel of Matthew

Enmity and hatred is cast among them that shall last until the day of Resurrection. But every time they kindle the fire of war, God shall extinguish it. Ever they seek to create disorder on earth: and God loves not those who create disorder.

ISLAMIC SCRIPTURES
Qu'ran, Sura 5

Peace is great because peace is to the earth what yeast is to bread. If the Holy One, blessed is He, had not given peace to the earth, swords and men, like the beasts of the fields, would destroy the world.

JEWISH TRADITION
The Talmud

Killing one man constitutes a crime and is punishable by death. Applying the same principle, the killing of ten men makes the crime ten times greater and ten times as punishable; similarly, the killing of a hundred men increases the evil a hundredfold, and makes it that many times as punishable.

All this the people of the world unanimously condemn and pronounce to be wrong. But when they come to judge the greatest of all wrongs—the invasion of one state by another—(which is a hundred thousand times more criminal than the killing of one innocent man) they cannot see that they should condemn it. On the contrary, they praise it and call it right. . . . Indeed, they do not *know* it is wrong.

Here is a world which condemns a petty wrong and praises the greatest of all wrongs—the attack of one nation on another—and calls it right. Can we say that the world knows the distinction between right and wrong?

CHINESE TRADITIONS
Words of Mo Ti

From whence come wars and fightings among you? Come they not hence, even of your lusts that war in your members? Ye lust, and have not: ye kill, and desire to have, and cannot obtain: yet fight and war, yet ye have not, because ye ask not.

CHRISTIAN SCRIPTURES
The Book of James

Then Arjuna saw standing there, ready for battle, uncles and grandfathers, teachers, mother's brothers, cousins, sons and grandsons, comrades, fathers-in-law, and bene-factors in both armies. Seeing his kinsmen thus arrayed, he was deeply moved to pity and cried out in sadness:

"O Krishna, seeing my kinsmen in battle dress, eager to fight, my limbs fail and my face withers, my body trembles and my hair stands on end. The Gandiva slips from my hand, my skin is aflame, I cannot stand up, my head is spinning. I see only bad omens, O long-haired one, and can find no good in slaying my kinsmen in battle.

"I desire no victory, O Krishna, nor my king-dom, nor its pleasures. What good is kingdom, or pleasures, or life? Those for whose sake we desired them stand here at war, abandoning life and riches—teachers, fathers, sons and grand-fathers, uncles, fathers-in-law, grandsons and brothers-in-law: kinsmen all. These I would not kill, though I myself be slain, O Madhusudana, for the rule of three worlds, much less for this earth.

"O Krishna, what pleasure can we find in slay-ing these sons of Dhritarashtra? Sin will take hold of us. We will not kill them, our brothers. For if we slay our own kin, how can we walk in joy, O Lord of Madhu?

"Those whose minds are overwhelmed by greed see no evil in destroying a family, no crime in attacking friends. But we see the evil clearly,

O Krishna, and will turn away from this guilt. When a family is destroyed, so perish its traditions and laws; when the traditions perish, lawlessness will come upon the whole race; when lawlessness comes upon us, our women will fall into sin; when the women are corrupted, society is confused; this confusion will bring both slayers and slain to hell, for their line will fall when their ancestors are forgotten. From the deeds of those who destroy a family, the ancient laws of the race and the family are lost. For those whose family customs are extinguished, O Krishna, a dwelling is ordained in hell. So we have heard.

"Alas! A great sin are we resolved to do, we who would kill our kindred because we lust after the pleasures of kingship. Even if the sons of Dhritarashtra will slay me with the weapons in their hands, it is better that I die unresisting and unarmed."

Having spoken these words on the battlefield, Arjuna sank to the seat of his chariot. He cast away his bow and arrow, and his mind was overcome with grief.

HINDU SCRIPTURES
The Bhagavad-Gita

The man of Tao who serves a ruler does not use weapons of force against the people. His acts are those that he would wish rendered to himself. Where armies are quartered, briars and thorns grow. In the wake of great armies, there will follow bad years.

TAOIST SCRIPTURES
Tao Te Ching

O Maker of the world! O Holy One! Where is the place where the Earth feels most happy?

Ahura Mazda answered: "It is the place where one of the faithful steps forward, O Zarathustra, . . . fulfilling the law with love, and beseeching aloud the Lord of wide pastures, the God that gives good folds and good pastures . . ."

O Maker of the World! O Holy One! Where is the place where the Earth feels deepest grief?

Ahura Mazda answered: "It is the place where the wife and children of one of the faithful slain in battle, O Zarathustra, are carried into slavery, and lift up their voices in wailing."

ZOROASTRIAN SCRIPTURES
The Zend-Avesta

War is the scourge of states, the tomb of justice. When the world is at arms, laws are reduced to silence. War encourages murder, opprobrium, adultery, incest. If impiety and forgetfulness of religion are causes of all evils, these two woes are brought to the last extremity by the cruelty of war. A state, we know, disintegrates when the evil have too much authority. In time of war, the evil reign as masters, and those who in times of peace would be put to death become the authors of the most remarkable exploits. . . .

Most of the people detest war and desire peace. A small number, whose accursed happiness always depends upon the misfortune of the common people, want war. Must their inhumanity outweigh the will of so many good people? Look to the past and see that up to now nothing has been definitely established, either by treaties or by family alliances, by force or by vengeance; nothing guarantees against danger so surely as kindness and good will. Wars lead to wars. Vengeance attracts vengeance. Indulgence creates indulgence. Good will invites to good will. Thus those who yield even a small part of their rights will enjoy the greatest consideration.

ERASMUS
Peace Protests, Sixteenth Century

War is destruction while universal peace is construction; war is death while peace is life; war is rapacity and bloodthirstiness while peace is beneficence and humaneness; war is an appurtenance of the world of nature while peace is of the foundation of the religion of God; war is darkness upon darkness while peace is heavenly light; war is the destroyer of the edifice of mankind while peace is the everlasting life of the world of humanity; war is like a devouring wolf while peace is like the angels of heaven; war is the struggle for existence while peace is mutual aid and co-operation among the peoples of the world and the cause of the good-pleasure of the True One in the heavenly realm.

There is not one soul whose conscience does not testify that in this day there is no more important matter in the world than that of universal peace.

'ABDU'L-BAHÁ
"Tablet to the Hague," 1919

War with all its glorification of brute force is essentially a degrading thing. It demoralizes those who are trained for it. It brutalizes men of naturally gentle character. It outrages every beautiful canon of morality. Its path of glory is foul with the passions of lust, and red with the blood of murder. This is not the pathway to our goal. The grandest aid to development of strong, pure, beautiful character, which is our aim, is the endurance of suffering, self-restraint, unselfishness, patience, gentleness: these are the flowers which spring beneath the feet of those who accept but refuse to impose suffering.

MOHANDAS GANDHI (1869–1948)

Every up-to-date dictionary should say that "peace" and "war" mean the same thing, now *in posse,* now *in actu.* It may even reasonably be said that the intense sharp competitive *preparation* for war by the nations *is the real war,* permanent, unceasing; and that the battles are only a sort of public verification of the mastery gained during the "peace"-interval.

WILLIAM JAMES
Moral Equivalent to War, 1910

In reality war is continuous. The moral effect of the expenditures of these colossal sums of money for military purposes is just as deteriorating as the actual war and its train of dreadful carnage and horrors. The ideal and moral forces of the contending parties become barbaric and bestial, the spiritual powers are stunted and the laws of divine civilization are disregarded. Such a financial drain ossifies the veins and muscles of the body-politic, and congeals the delicate sensibilities of the spirit.

There is not the least doubt that the nation or the government which puts forward an extraordinary effort in the promotion of Universal Peace, will be enriched with Divine Confirmations, and will be the object of honor and respect among all the inhabitants of the earth.

'ABDU'L-BAHÁ
"Questions and Answers," 1919

Tell General Howard I know his heart. What he told me before I have in my heart. I am tired of fighting. Our chiefs are killed.

Looking Glass is dead. Tuhulhulsote is dead. The old men are all dead. It is the young men who say yes or no in the councils. He who was the leader of the young men is dead. It is cold and we have no blankets. The little children are freezing to death. My people, some of them, have run away to the hills, and have no blankets, no food; no one knows where they are—perhaps freezing to death. I want to have time to look for my children and see how many of them I can find. Maybe I shall find them among the dead. Hear me, my chiefs. I am tired; my heart is sick and sad. From where the sun now stands I will fight no more forever.

NATIVE AMERICAN
Chief Joseph (Nez Perce)
Surrender Speech, 1877

It is reported that two kingdoms were on the verge of war, the possession of a certain area of land being disputed by them. Then the Buddha, seeing the kings with their armies ready to fight, requested them to tell him the cause of their quarrels.

Having heard the complaints on both sides, he said: "I understand that the land has value for some of your people. Has it any intrinsic value aside from its service to your men?"

"It has no intrinsic value whatever," was the reply.

The Buddha continued: "Now when you go into battle, is it not certain that many of your men will be slain, and you yourselves, O kings, are liable to lose your lives?"

And they said, "Yes, it is sure that many will perish, and our own lives will be in jeopardy."

"The blood of men, however," said the Buddha, "has it less intrinsic value than a mound of earth?"

"No," the kings answered, "the lives of men, and above that the lives of kings, are priceless."

Then the Buddha concluded, "Are you going to sacrifice that which is priceless for that which has no intrinsic value at all?" And the wrath of the two monarchs abated, and they came to a peaceful agreement.

BUDDHIST TRADITION
Words of the Buddha

Peace: The Inner Struggle

Seeing the crowds, he went up on the mountain, and when he sat down his disciples came to him. And he opened his mouth and taught them, saying:

"Blessed are the poor in spirit, for theirs is the kingdom of heaven.

"Blessed are those who mourn, for they shall be comforted.

"Blessed are the meek, for they shall inherit the earth.

"Blessed are those who hunger and thirst for righteousness, for they shall be satisfied.

"Blessed are the merciful, for they shall obtain mercy.

"Blessed are the pure in heart, for they shall see God.

"Blessed are the peacemakers, for they shall be called sons of God."

CHRISTIAN SCRIPTURES
The Gospel of Matthew

The man thinks that war against his weaker opponents will bring victory. But lacking in righteousness, he fails in his endeavors. Returning from the path of strife to one of inner harmony with the eternal law, he finds peace and good fortune.

CHINESE TRADITIONS
I Ching

When a man surrenders all desires that come to the heart and by the grace of God finds the joy of God, then his soul has indeed found Peace.

HINDU SCRIPTURES
The Bhagavad-Gita

The first peace, which is the most important, is that which comes within the souls of men when they realize their relationship, their oneness, with the universe and all its powers, and when they realize that at the center of the universe dwells *Wakan-Tanka,* and that this center is really everywhere, it is within each of us. This is the real Peace, and the others are but reflections of this. The second peace is that which is made between two individuals, and the third is that which is made between two nations. But above all you should understand that there can never be peace between nations until there is first known that true peace which, as I have often said, is within the souls of men.

> NATIVE AMERICAN
> Black Elk (Oglala Sioux)
> *The Sacred Pipe,* 1953

If you want to see the brave, look at those who can forgive. If you want to see the heroic, look at those who can love in return for hatred.

> HINDU SCRIPTURES
> The Bhagavad-Gita

You have heard that it was said, "You shall love your neighbor and hate your enemy." But I say to you, Love your enemies and pray for those who persecute you, so that you may be sons of your Father who is in heaven; for he makes his sun rise on the evil and on the good, and sends rain on the just and on the unjust. For if you love those who love you, what reward have you? Do not even the tax collectors do the same? And if you salute only your breathren, what more are you doing than others?

CHRISTIAN SCRIPTURES
The Gospel of Matthew

O Friend!
In the garden of thy heart plant naught but the rose of love, and from the nightingale of affection and desire loosen not thy hold . . .

BAHÁ'Í SCRIPTURES
The Hidden Words of Bahá'u'lláh

Mutual love is righteousness, but warfare is unrighteousness. The former is beneficial to Heaven, spirit, country, and humanity—the latter means destruction to all.

CHINESE TRADITIONS
Words of Mo Ti

If I speak in the tongues of men and of angels, but have not love, I am a noisy gong or a clanging cymbal. And if I have prophetic powers, and understand all mysteries and all knowledge, and if I have all faith, so as to remove mountains, but have not love, I am nothing. If I give away all I have, and if I deliver my body to be burned, but have not love, I gain nothing.

Love is patient and kind; love is not jealous or boastful; it is not arrogant or rude. Love does not insist on its own way; it is not irritable or resentful; it does not rejoice at wrong, but rejoices in the right. Love bears all things, believes all things, hopes all things, endures all things.

Love never ends . . .

So faith, hope, love abide, these three; but the greatest of these is love.

CHRISTIAN SCRIPTURES
St. Paul, I Corinthians

I stand against all learning, all institutions, all governments, all arts, all religions, which reject love. I protest against every so-called church which preaches faith and fails to love. I oppose the politicians who rely on force and know nothing about love. If I have to be arrested for saying this, let me be handcuffed, for I had rather die quickly by the sword than die of thirst in a loveless desert. . . .

Love evolves perennially, never grudging sacrifice. Since love has never abhorred martyrdom, it perceives that in the process of evolution it is more effective to be killed than to kill.

Men who fear to make the sacrifice of love will have to fight. Those who believe in the sacrifice through love believe in the principle of noninjury.

For those who eternally evolve, there is an eternal cross.

Love is basic for the birth of a true society, while violence has in it the essence of anti-sociality.

Love is positive; violence is negative.

Love injures none, is eternal. Violence is degeneracy: it is its own destruction.

TOYOHIKO KAGAWA (1888–1960)

The invincible weapon, always victorious, is the incessant act of love.

SISTER CONSALATA
Seventeenth Century

I say to you, Do not resist one who is evil. But if any one strikes you on the right cheek, turn to him the other also; and if any one would sue you and take your coat, let him have your cloak as well; and if any one forces you to go one mile, go with him two miles. Give to him who begs from you, and do not refuse him who would borrow from you.

CHRISTIAN SCRIPTURES
The Gospel of Matthew

Our truth is an ancient one: That love endures and overcomes; that hatred destroys; that what is obtained by love is retained, but what is obtained by hatred proves a burden.

AMERICAN FRIENDS SERVICE COMMITTEE
Speak Truth To Power

A man finds no justice if he carries a dispute to violence. No, he who knows right from wrong, who is learned and guides others—not by violence, but by the same law, being a guardian of the law, who shows intelligence: he is called just.

BUDDHIST SCRIPTURES
The Dhammapada

Fighting, and the employment of force, even for the right cause, will not bring good results.

'ABDU'L-BAHÁ
Tablets of 'Abdu'l-Bahá, 1909

Thou shalt not kill.

JEWISH SCRIPTURES
The Book of Exodus

This is the quintessence of wisdom: not to kill anything. Know this to be the legitimate conclusion from the principle of reciprocity with regard to nonkilling. He should cease to injure living beings whether they move or not, on high, below, and on earth. For this has been called Nirvana, which consists of peace.

JAIN SCRIPTURES
The Sutrakritanga

All fear violence. All fear death. One should compare onself to others, and should neither kill nor cause to be killed.

All fear violence. All love live. One should compare oneself to others, and should neither kill nor cause to be killed.

Whoever harms another being, seeking his own happiness, will find no happiness hereafter. But whoever, seeking happiness, harms no other being will find happiness hereafter . . .

He who harms the harmless and defenseless, soon will come to no good: He will suffer pain, disaster, injury, or sickness; loss of mind, oppression, accusation; or loss of loved ones, or loss of wealth, or a ravaging fire that will burn his house. And after death, this foolish man will be reborn in hell.

BUDDHIST SCRIPTURES
The Dhammapada

Men cannot be our enemies—even men called 'Vietcong!'
If we kill men, what brothers will we have left? With whom shall we live then?

Even as they
strike you down
with a mountain of hate and violence . . .
remember brother,
remember,
man is not our enemy.

THICH NHAT HANH
Vietnamese Buddhist

You have heard that it was said to men of old, "You shall not kill; and whoever kills shall be liable to judgment." But I say to you that every one who is angry with his brother shall be liable to judgment; whoever insults his brother shall be liable to the council, and whoever says, "You fool!" shall be liable to the hell of fire.

CHRISTIAN SCRIPTURES
The Gospel of Matthew

Let a man leave behind all anger, let him forsake pride, let him overcome all bondage! No suffering befalls a man who is not attached to name and form, and who calls nothing his own.

He who holds back his anger like a rolling chariot, I call him the real driver. Others only hold the reins.

Overcome anger by love; overcome evil by good; overcome greed by generosity; and the lie by truth! Speak the truth and do not yield to anger; give if you are asked, and by these steps you will go near the gods.

BUDDHIST SCRIPTURES
Pali Texts

A man said to the Prophet, "Give me a command." He said, "Let nothing provoke thee to anger." The man said to the Prophet, "Give another command." And he replied, "Let nothing provoke thee to anger." The man repeated the question several times, and the

Prophet said, "Let nothing provoke thee to anger."

ISLAMIC TRADITION
Words of Muhammad

Happily do we live without hate, amongst the hateful. We dwell with hateful men and hate not. . . . Victory begets hatred, and the defeated live in pain. Happily do we live as peaceful beings, renouncing victory and defeat.

There is no fire greater than longing, no greater crime than hate. There is no greater evil than form, and no greater bliss than Peace.

BUDDHIST SCRIPTURES
The Dhammapada

Let man find the path of the Spirit: who has found this path becomes free from the bonds of evil. Who knows this has found peace; he is the lord of himself; his is a calm endurance, and calm concentration.

HINDU SCRIPTURES
The Upanishads

But the wisdom from above is pure, first of all; it is also peaceful, gentle, and friendly; it is full of compassion and produces a harvest of good deeds; it is free from prejudice and hypocrisy. And goodness is the harvest that is produced from the seeds the peacemakers plant in peace.

CHRISTIAN SCRIPTURES
The Book of James

O Lord, our Christ, may we have thy mind and thy spirit; make us instruments of thy peace; where there is hatred, let us sow love; where there is injury, pardon; where there is discord, union; where there is doubt, faith; where there is despair, hope; where there is darkness, light; and where there is sadness, joy. O divine Master, grant that we may not so much seek to be consoled as to console; to be understood, as to understand; to be loved, as to love; for it is in giving that we receive, it is in pardoning that we are pardoned, and it is in dying that we are born to eternal life. Amen.

ST. FRANCIS OF ASSISI
Thirteenth Century

Shall I not tell you what is better than prayers and fasting and giving alms to the poor? It is making peace between one another: enmity and malice destroy all virtues.

ISLAMIC TRADITION
Words of Muhammad

I charge you all that each one of you concentrate all the thoughts of your heart on love and unity. When a thought of war comes, oppose it by a stronger thought of peace. A thought of hatred must be destroyed by a more powerful thought of love. Thoughts of war bring destruction to all harmony, well-being, restfulness and content . . . Thoughts of love are constructive of brotherhood, peace, friendship, and happiness.

'ABDU'L-BAHÁ
Paris Talks, 1911

Waging Peace

As long as I have will and am physically
  capable,
So long will I teach mankind
To strive for truth, order and peace.

ZOROASTRIAN SCRIPTURES
The Yasna

The ancients, when they wished
to exemplify illustrious virtue throughout the
empire, first brought peace and order to their
states. Desiring to bring peace and order to their
states, they first brought the same to their families. Wishing to bring peace to their families,
they first cultivated themselves. Wishing to
cultivate themselves, they first purified their
purposes. Wishing to purify their purposes, they
first sought to think sincerely. Wishing to think
sincerely, they first extended their knowledge as

widely as possible. They did this by the investigation of all things.

By investigation of things, their knowledge became extensive; their knowledge being extensive, their thoughts became sincere; their thoughts being sincere, their purposes were rectified; their purposes being rectified, they cultivated themselves; having cultivated themselves, their families were regulated; their families having been regulated, their states were governed rightly; their states being rightly governed, the empire was thereby brought to peace and prosperity.

CONFUCIAN SCRIPTURES
Words of Confucius

Let us therefore follow after the things which make for peace . . .

CHRISTIAN SCRIPTURES
The Book of Romans

If your enemy should incline to peace,
Do thou incline to peace also,
And trust in God:
For He is the Hearing, the All-Knowing.

ISLAMIC SCRIPTURES
Qu'ran, Sura 8

Woe is me . . .
Too long have I had my dwelling
    among those who hate peace.
I am for peace;
    but when I speak,
    they are for war!

JEWISH SCRIPTURES
The Psalms

We should be innocent not only of violence but of all enmity, however slight, for this is the mystery of peace.

ST. JOHN CHRYSOSTOM
Fourth Century

Finally, *peace rests largely in the fact of desiring it with all the force of our soul.* Indeed, those who desire it grasp every occasion which is favorable to it. They disregard certain justified claims, smooth over difficulties which oppose it, even endure disagreeable things in order to save that great good which is peace. Unfortunately, it is the opposite that happens. We see today—I will not wear myself out repeating it—princes carefully seeking excuses for war. They suppress and hide everything that might maintain peace; they exaggerate excessively, and to the point of exasperation, everything that would lead to an outbreak of war.

ERASMUS
Peace Protests, Sixteenth Century

Inner peace comes from binding (*religio*) to God. . . . But this inner peace must not lead to inaction. It must be tied with a movement, a necessary unrest, which leads us to action. It is distinguished from the frantic movement of fear and anxiety; it is a movement still bound to God. The greatest mystics, even in their times of ecstasy, felt the need to return to the needs of the world.

MARGARETHE LACHMUND
Quaker, 1958

To work for peace means to work for one's own liberation, and vice versa. This condition of working, struggling, organizing —in a word, *life*—Jesus, in the Sermon on the Mount, calls by an old word, "Blessed." "Happy are the peacemakers." Unhappy are those who don't take part. Those who work for peace are "blessed" now, not just later. Even when we experience defeat, we come into a condition where we don't regret anything anymore.

DOROTHEE SOLLE
"Peace Needs Women," 1983

A himsa is not merely nonparticipation in destructive activities; it principally manifests itself in constructive activities—services which lead to the upward growth of man. People say that the Goddess of Ahimsa has no weapons; I say that is wrong. The Goddess of Ahimsa has very powerful weapons at her command. They are the weapons of love and are, therefore, creative and not destructive. Yet they do destroy; they destroy hatred, inequity, hunger, and disease. It is true, however, that the weapons of *ahimsa* look small in size and slow in action . . .

The light of *ahimsa* cannot be spread by the external and formal mechanism of organizations. History shows that Jesus came alone and the light that he brought pervaded the world—not through church institutions or "Christian" governments, but in spite of them. The light inspires us even today. The same is true of the Buddha. He was a prince but his message could not be spread by the authority of the state. It spread because he threw his kingdom away like a wisp of straw.

After all, what is it that will spread nonviolence? It is not the body that can do it, for the body is an embodiment of violence. *Ahimsa* is assimilated to the extent one rises above one's body. Nonviolence is the natural state of the soul.

What *ahimsa,* therefore, needs is the quest of the spirit, the purification of the mind, service of living creatures, love universal and fearlessness.

> VINOBA BHAVE
> "The True Nature of Ahimsa and Our Duty," 1949

Nonviolence is a weapon fabricated of love. It is a sword that heals. Our nonviolent direct action program has as its objective not the creation of tensions, but the surfacing of tensions already present. We set out to precipitate a crisis situation that must open the door to negotiation. I am not afraid of the words "crisis" and "tension." I deeply oppose violence, but constructive crisis and tension are necessary for growth. Innate in all life, and all growth, is tension. Only in death is there an absence of tension.

MARTIN LUTHER KING, JR. (1929–1968)

The warfare is spiritual, and to spiritual conflict we must bring spiritual weapons . . . One of the essential elements is prayer. Unfortunately, prayer is often the last thing that many who work for peace think of. But peacemaking reflects the heart and the will of the Father and is not simply the activity of a few interested individuals. To be a peacemaker is to begin by praying for peace.

What can we expect God to do when we pray for peace? There was a time when I expected those prayers to be answered by the Lord's simply putting an end to the fighting, stopping the wars, and reducing the overall level of violence in our society. I assumed that I would be a spectator, watching the process from the sidelines. But that kind of picture belongs to a fantasy world, a make-believe universe.

The Hebrew word *shalom*, which we generally translate as "peace," is a far richer word than its English equivalent. It means much more than the absence of conflict. It means the presence of those just and equitable relationships between people, and between people and the Lord, which one might describe as a condition of total well-being for all. Or to put it another way, if peace means the absence of conflict, then it also means the elimination of all those factors that produce

44

conflict and the establishment of the kind of just and equitable society where conflict is unnecessary. In shalom, our two initial concerns of peacemaking and feeding the hungry become almost synonymous.

To pray for peace means to pray for a rearrangement of some of the pieces of our own life, an alteration in our life-style and standard of living. It is to ask the Lord to take away some of our toys, particularly those which consume so much fossil-fuel energy. It is to ask the Lord to reduce our surplus in order that other people and nations might simply have enough. We cannot call that state of affairs peace where the starving are asked to keep quiet so as not to disturb the sleep of the overfed. To pray for peace means to pray for the removal of those malignancies which hinder the world's health.

Prayer and action belong together. Someone remarked that action without prayer is presumptuous, but prayer without action is blasphemous. How then can we act as peacemakers?

New Testament teaching and human experience agree that we should begin with the smaller things before tackling the larger ones. When asked for some life-changing advice by a journalist, Mother Teresa replied, "Smile at the people you live with!" We will try peacemaking with those we live and work with before attempting it on an international scale. And we might try to convert the Christian church before we try the Pentagon and the Kremlin.

WILLIAM C. FREY
Rumors of War, 1982

All who believe in some kind of moral order, whether or not they are Christians or consider themselves religious at all, face a crucial problem in connection with war. The question is not whether one is going to die in war; at the appointed time all men, and nations also, die. This is in the order of nature. The question for the morally responsible being is what happens to *himself* if he becomes a murderer, drops atomic bombs on little enemy children instead of trying to bring them food and healing. The question is what *moral* price he is prepared to pay for his country's victory in war . . .

The morally responsible person . . . has to be true, in the final pinch, to the highest that he knows. He has to be able to live with himself. If his moral standard amounts to obeying whatever orders some government gives him (remember the Nuremberg doctrine of the guilt of *individual* Nazis) or if his standard is what he can get away with, then he is no longer a moral being. This is why, in fact, any human being not bereft of sanity altogether "draws a line somewhere," at some point says, "I can do no other."

A. J. MUSTE
Non-violence in an
Aggressive World, 1954

The horror and evil of war cannot be conquered by the anaemic gospel of pacifism, which is generally connected with abstract cosmopolitanism. Pacifism is the opposite of militarism, but there is no final moral truth in either. Pacifism is optimistic and ignores the tragic nature of history. There is a certain amount of truth in it—the will, namely, that wars should cease. But pacifism does not recognize the spiritual conditions needed to end wars; it remains on the surface, in the domain of unreal politics and legal formulae, unconscious of the irrational forces at work in the world. Pacifism is a form of rationalism. The preaching of peace and of the brotherhood of nations is a Christian work, and Christian ethics must take it over from rationalistic pacifism. For Christian consciousness the problem is complicated by the understanding of the evil and irrational forces of history.

War has a fatal dialectic of its own which will bring it to an end sooner than the preaching of peace. War is connected with the development of technical sciences. Recent discoveries of new means of attack and destruction are so monstrous that they must lead to the self-negation of war and make it impossible . . . The chivalrous aspects of war connected with courage, manliness, honour and loyalty are disappearing and losing their significance. They played hardly any part in the last war. War is becoming quite a different kind of thing and requires another name. War will be destroyed by the technique of war. The question of the spiritual and moral communion of nations thus becomes the question of the further existence of mankind, which is threatened with destruction through the new and more perfect means of warfare. . . .

We are entering an epoch when war loses meaning and can be no longer justifed, and when

struggle against the possibility of new wars becomes a sacred obligation.

NICOLAS BERDYAEV
The Destiny of Man, 1955

The ideals of Peace must be
nurtured and spread among the inhabitants of the
world; they must be instructed in the school of
Peace and the evils of war. First: The financiers
and bankers must desist from lending money to
any government contemplating to wage an unjust
war upon an innocent nation. Second: The presi-
dents and managers of the railroads and steam-
ship companies must refrain from transporting
war ammunition, infernal engines, guns, cannons
and powder from one country into another. Third:
The soldiers must petition, through their representatives, the Ministers of War, the politicians,
the Congressmen and the generals to put forth in
a clear, intelligible language the reasons and
the causes which have brought them to the brink
of such a national calamity. The soldiers must
demand this as one of their prerogatives. "Demon-

strate to us," they must say, "that this is a just war, and we will then enter into the battlefield otherwise we will not take one step. O ye kings and rulers, politicians and warmongers; ye who spend your lives in most exquisite palaces of Italian architecture; ye who sleep in airy, well-ventilated apartments; ye who decorate your reception and dining halls with lovely pictures, sculptures, hangings and frescoes; ye who walk in perfect elysiums, wreathed in orange and myrtle groves, the air redolent with delicious perfumes and vocal with the sweet songs of a thousand birds, the earth like a luxuriant carpet of emerald grass, bright flowers dotting the meadows and trees clothed in verdure; ye who are dressed in costly silk and finely-woven textures; ye who lie down on soft, feathery couches; ye who partake of the most delicious and savoury dishes; ye who enjoy the utmost ease and comfort in your wondrous mansions; ye who attend rare musical concerts whenever you feel a little disconcerted and sad; ye who adorn your large halls with green festoons and cut flowers, fresh garlands and verdant wreaths, illuminating them with thousands of electric lights, while the exquisite fragrance of the flowers, the soft, ravishing music, the fairy-like illumination, lends enchantment; ye who are in such environment: Come forth from your hiding-places, enter into the battlefield if you like to attack each other and tear each other to pieces if you desire to air your so-called contentions. The discord and feud are between you; why do you make us, innocent people, a party to it? If fighting and bloodshed are good things, then lead us into the fray by your presence!"

In short, every means that produces war must be checked and the causes that prevent the occurrence of war be advanced;—so that physical conflict may become an impossibility. On the other hand, every country must be properly delimited, its exact frontiers marked, its national integrity secured, its permanent independence protected, and its vital interests honored by the family of nations. These services ought to be rendered by an impartial, international Commission. In this manner all causes of friction and differences will be removed. And in case there should arise some disputes between them, they could arbitrate before the Parliament of Man, the representatives of which should be chosen from among the wisest and most judicious men of all the nations of the world.

'ABDU'L-BAHÁ
"Questions and Answers," 1914

When conscientious and politically sane citizens refuse to render a service to the state which used to be considered a very real service, but has now, in their opinion, become politically useless, they show political wisdom; this is shown by the fact that they regard this refusal as the command of God to them, not in the legalistic sense of fanatics, but in the concrete sense of political responsibility—that is, in a quite different sense from those who refuse this service simply on the ground of the command: "Thou shalt not kill," or on the basis of the Sermon on the Mount. They will bear witness to this new point of view by taking without complaint the punishment imposed upon them by the state, knowing well that the state does not yet see what they see, and thus that it regards what they are doing as service to the state as "a refusal to serve."

When a new order is struggling to come into being and to shake off the shackles of the old order, the idea of order itself begins to waver, and this leads to hesitation about the ethical obligation of obedience to the state. An ethical right to revolution which can be expressed in general terms does not exist; but the necessity does arise of making a choice between the new order which is coming into being and the old order which is falling into decay. Even the Christian cannot evade this necessity, for no one can. Where the old order no longer performs its service of providing for order a new order is necessary, whose "tragedy" consists in the fact that it must first of all do away with the old "order," that it may establish real order in place of a sham order. In itself it is impossible to justify revolution from the ethical point of view even when it takes place for the sake of a better order, for it elevates anarchy to the level of a principle, and in so doing it destroys the basis of all morality. But just as the duty of obedience to the state is always qualified by obedience to God's command, so also it is qualified by the possibility that God intends to destroy the old order because it has degenerated into a sham. But only unavoidable necessity will avail to protect this dangerous action from the reproach of rebellion against God.

EMIL BRUNNER
The Divine Imperative, 1947

Physical conflict is marked by the risk and sacrifice of life. Without sacrifice there is no human existence. Today we have two choices: either the sacrifice—unwanted by the overwhelming majority, accomplished by the daring minority—is *the existence* of mankind itself, doomed because man cannot be free; or mankind sacrifices *the means of force* in gaining its ends in a struggle. But that would mean a change in man, not in his inheritable constitution, but in his historic appearance, in the steadily imperiled balance of his being.

We may ask: Must man be able to risk everything, even the existence of mankind, to become serious enough to change? Is a new humankind to spring from the awareness of this possibly total risk and from the readiness for it? Or, if the change does not take place, shall all be doomed? Shall mankind perish if it finds no way to realize justice in a moral-political community? And if no such way is found, does the substance of humanity then lie where failure is no longer an objection—where indeed man's ultimately real, truly serious purpose is his doom?

We can raise that question, but no one can answer it. We have only mythical answers from prehistoric times, as when God sent the Flood. When the wickedness of men waxed too great, he resolved to let them perish as no longer fit to live.

We have had the Flood, but we also have had Noah's rescue. And in the end, God promised never to repeat it.

Goethe said of the dawning modern age: "Mankind will grow more astute and more perceptive, but not better, happier, or more vigorous—not permanently, at least. I see a time coming when God will not enjoy it any more, when he will have to smash everything once again, to rejuvenate his creation. I feel sure that everything tends in that direction, and that the starting time and hour of rejuvenation period are already appointed in the distant future. But there will be plenty of time yet."

These mythical notions have acts of God in mind, but today the issue is not a cosmic disaster but an act accomplished by the technical skills of men. If their doings would result in self-extermination, only their doings can avoid it. In any event, the gate to the future is sacrifice—either the sacrifice of all human existence or the sacrifice of human existential interests, offered to let mankind become truly human. . . .

Because there is truth in serious, unconditional resistance to the abasement of life, the chance of sacrifice—not adequately justifiable by any purpose in the world, but based upon reason by a goal in the situation of the world—is part of man. If we must do everything to eliminate the atom bomb, the condition is that it not be done at the cost of eliminating a truly human life. The sacrifice of mankind's existence is avoidable only by a sacrifice of corresponding magnitude: by the surrender of existential entanglements that is required if men are to be changed. This sacrifice alone would be the firm foundation of a life worth living.

KARL JASPERS
Future of Mankind, 1965

The village of Le Chambon sur Lignon collectively sheltered and saved the lives of many hundreds of Jews through the years when the penalty for this crime was deportation or death. The villagers were led by the Protestant pastor, André Trocmé, who had been for many years a believer in nonviolence and had prepared them mentally and spiritually for this trial of strength. When the Gestapo from time to time raided the village, Trocmé's spies usually gave him enough warning so that the refugees could be hidden in the woods. German authorities arrested and executed various people who were known to

be leaders in the village, but the resistance continued unbroken. The only way the Germans
could have crushed the resistance was by deport-
ing or killing the entire population. Nearby, in the
same region of France, there was a famous regi-
ment of SS troops, the Tartar Legion, trained and
experienced in operations of extermination and
mass brutality. The Tartar Legion could easily
have exterminated Le Chambon. But the village
survived. Even Trocmé himself, by a series of
lucky accidents, survived.

Many years later, Trocmé discovered how it
happened that the village survived. The fate of
the village was decided in a dialogue between two
German soldiers, representing the bright and the
dark sides of the German soul. On the one side,
Colonel Metzger, an appropriate name meaning
in German "butcher," commander of the Tartar
Legion, killer of civilians, executed after the liberation of France as a war criminal. On the other
side, Major Schmehling, Bavarian Catholic and
decent German officer of the old school. Both
Metzger and Schmehling were present at the trial
of Le Forestier, a medical doctor in Le Chambon
who was arrested and executed as an example to
the villagers. "At his trial," said Schmehling
when he met Trocmé many years later, "I heard
the words of Dr. Le Forestier, who was a Christian and explained to me very clearly why you

were disobeying all our orders at Le Chambon. I believed that your doctor was sincere. I am a good Catholic, you understand, and I can grasp these things. . . . Well, Colonel Metzger was a hard one, and he kept on insisting that we move in on Le Chambon. But I kept telling him to wait. I told Metzger that this kind of resistance had nothing to do with violence, nothing to do with anything we could destroy with violence. With all my personal and military power I opposed sending his legion into Le Chambon.''

That was how it worked. It was a wonderful illustration of the classic concept of nonviolent resistance. You, Dr. Le Forestier, die for your beliefs, apparently uselessly. But your death reaches out and touches your enemies, so that they begin to behave like human beings. Some of your enemies, like Major Schmehling, are converted into friends. And finally even the most hardened and implacable of your enemies, like the SS colonel, are persuaded to stop their killing. It happened like that, once upon a time, in Le Chambon.

What did it take to make the concept of nonviolent resistance effective? It took a whole village of people, standing together with extraordinary courage and extraordinary discipline. Not all of them shared the religious faith of their leader, but all of them shared his moral convictions and risked their lives every day to make their village a place of refuge for the persecuted. They were united in friendship, loyalty, and respect for one another.

Sooner or later, everybody who thinks seriously about the meaning of nuclear weapons and nuclear war must face the question whether nonviolence is or is not a practical alternative to the path we are now following. Is nonviolence a possible basis for the foreign policy of a great country like the United States? Or is it only a private escape route available to religious minorities who are protected by a majority willing to fight for their lives? I do not know the answers to these questions. I do not think that anybody knows the answers. The example of Le Chambon shows us that we cannot in good conscience brush such accusations aside. . . . Can we conceive of the population of the United States standing together in brotherhood and self-sacrifice like the villagers of Le Chambon? It is difficult to imagine any circumstances which would make this possible. But history teaches us that many things which were once unimaginable nevertheless came to pass. At the end of every discussion of nonviolence comes the question which Bernard Shaw put at the end of his play *Saint Joan:*

O God that madest this beautiful earth, when will it be ready to receive Thy Saints? How long, O Lord, how long?

FREEMAN DYSON
Weapons and Hope, 1984

Peace . . . is not a purely ideal dream, nor is it an attractive but fruitless and unattainable Utopia. It is, and must be, a reality —a dynamic reality and one to be generated at every stage of civilization, like the bread on which we live, the fruit of the earth and of divine Providence, but also the product of human work. In the same way, peace is not a state of public indifference in which those who enjoy it are dispensed from every care and defended from all disturbance and can permit themselves a stable and tranquil bliss savoring more of inertia and hedonism than of vigilant and diligent vigor. Peace is an equilibrium that is based on motion and continually gives forth energy of spirit and action; it is intelligent and living courage.

POPE PAUL VI
Day of Peace Message, 1978

Peace Out of Justice

More knowledge, more life.
More justice, more peace.

JEWISH TRADITION
The Talmud

We worship the Spirits of the Virtuous to withstand the wrong done by the oppressors who corrupt power and authority; to withstand the wrong done by the dead-in-conscience who forget the social good; and to withstand the wrong done by those yielding to passion, wrath, war, and violence.

ZOROASTRIAN SCRIPTURES
The Yasht

Let me hear the words of the Lord:
are they not words of peace,
  peace to his people and his loyal servants
  and to all who turn and trust in him?

Deliverance is near to those who worship him,
  so that glory may dwell in our land.
Love and fidelity have come together;
justice and peace join hands.

JEWISH SCRIPTURES
The Psalms

Whoever can protest against the injustices of his family but refrains from doing so, should be punished for the crimes of his family. Whoever can protest against the injustices of the people of his community, but refrains from doing so, should be punished for the crimes of his community. Whoever is able to protest against the injustices of the entire world but refrains from doing so, should be punished for the crimes of the whole world.

JEWISH TRADITION
The Talmud

The Spirit of the Lord is upon me,
because he has annointed me to preach good
  news to the poor.
He has sent me to proclaim release to the
  captives
and recovering of sight to the blind,
to set at liberty those who are oppressed,
to proclaim the acceptable year of the Lord.

CHRISTIAN SCRIPTURES
The Gospel of Luke

There is no better ruler than Wisdom, no safer guardian than Justice, no stronger sword than Righteousness, no surer ally than Truth.

ISLAMIC TRADITION
Words of Muhammad

To enjoy the benefits of providence is wisdom; to enable others to enjoy them is virtue. He who is indifferent to the welfare of others does not deserve to be called human. The best way to worship God is to ease the distress of the times and to improve the condition of humanity. This is true religion; to cleanse oneself with pure thoughts, pure words, and pure deeds.

ZOROASTRIAN SCRIPTURES
The Zend-Avesta

Take away from me the noise of your songs; to the melody of your harps I will not listen. But let justice roll down like waters, and righteousness like an everflowing stream.

JEWISH SCRIPTURES
The Book of Amos

O Son of Spirit!
The best beloved of all things in My sight is
Justice, turn not away therefrom if thou desirest
Me, and neglect it not that I may confide in thee.
By its aid thou shalt see with thine own eyes and
not through the eyes of others, and shalt know of
thine own knowledge and not through the knowledge of thy neighbor. Ponder this in thy heart;
how it behooveth thee to be. Verily justice is
My gift to thee and the sign of My loving-kind-
ness. Set it then before thine eyes.

BAHÁ'Í SCRIPTURES
The Hidden Words of Bahá'u'lláh

Would that even today you
know the things that make for peace.

CHRISTIAN SCRIPTURES
The Gospel of Luke

True peace is not merely the absence of tension; it is the presence of justice.

MARTIN LUTHER KING, JR. (1929–1968)

Peace among peoples requires: Truth as its foundation, justice as its rule, love as its driving force, liberty as its atmosphere.

CARDINAL SUENENS
United Nations Address, 1963

Recompense to no man evil for evil. Provide things honest in the sight of all men. If it be possible, as much as lieth in you, live peaceably with all men. Dearly beloved, avenge not yourselves, but rather give place unto wrath: for it is written, Vengeance is mine; I will repay, saith the Lord. Therefore if thine enemy hunger, feed him; if he thirst, give him drink: for in so doing thou shalt heap coals of fire on his head. Be not overcome of evil, but overcome evil with good.

CHRISTIAN SCRIPTURES
The Book of Romans

A pacifism which can see the cruelties only of occasional military warfare and is blind to the continuous cruelties of our social system is worthless. Unless our pacifism finds expression in the broad human movement which is seeking not merely the end of war but our equally non-pacifist civilization as a whole, it will be of little account in the onward march of mankind. The spirit of life will sweep on, quite uninfluenced by it.

Immediately after the spirit of exploitation is gone armaments will be felt as a positively unbearable burden. Real disarmament cannot come unless the nations of the world cease to exploit one another.

MOHANDAS GANDHI (1869–1948)

Peace is not simply the absence of war, a nuclear stalemate or combination of uneasy cease-fires. It is that emerging dynamic reality envisioned by prophets where spears and swords give way to implements of peace; where historic antagonists dwell together in trust; and where righteousness and justice prevail. There will be no peace with justice until unselfish and informed love are structured into political processes and international arrangements.

THE UNITED METHODIST CHURCH
adopted by the General Conference, 1980

It must however be stated quite clearly and without compromise that the duty of the Christian as a peacemaker is not to be confused with a kind of quietistic inertia that is indifferent to injustice, accepts any kind of disorder, compromises with error and with evil, and gives in to every pressure in order to maintain "peace at any price." The Christian knows well, or should know well, that peace is not possible on such terms. Peace demands the most heroic labor and the most difficult sacrifice. It demands greater heroism than war. It demands greater fidelity to the truth and a much more perfect purity of conscience.

THOMAS MERTON
"The Christian in World Crisis," 1961

The growing reality of mass hunger alongside the growing affluence of military states emphasizes the impotence of destructive power to effect any truly human change in the world, and the guilt of those who choose impotence. The power of the affluent not only threatens global destruction but actually carries it out in widening circles of famine and destitution. The jealous possession of such power renders man powerless to make peace both because it commits him to the end of all peace on earth and because it already wages global war against the hungry.

To the man of conscience, as defined by his sense of humanity, the growing fact of such a world raises the moral imperatives of resistance and revolution. Any political or economic system which can preach an ideological crusade against the poor, punctuating it with napalm and TNT, or can tolerate worms in the stomachs of children, deserves not allegiance but uprooting. To the human family's threatened murder by nuclear weapons and to its ongoing murder by privilege and indifference, the response of human conscience is "No!" In such a world, revolution is not a question and a possibility. It is an obligation and a necessity. One must either revolt against the disorder of the present system, for the sake of each man's right to the means of a human life, or cease being human oneself. The process of inhumanity and slow murder has already gone too far to allow an intermediate choice.

JAMES DOUGLASS
The Non-Violent Cross, 1968

A religion true to its nature must . . . be concerned about man's social conditions. Religion deals with both earth and heaven, both time and eternity. Any religion that professes to be concerned about the souls of men and is not concerned about the slums that damn them, the economic conditions that strangle them and the social conditions that cripple them is a dry-as-dust religion.

MARTIN LUTHER KING, JR. (1929–1968)

Banning nuclear weapons, prohibiting the use of poison gases, or outlawing germ warfare will not remove the root causes of war. However important such practical measures obviously are as elements of the peace process, they are in themselves too superficial to exert enduring influence. People are ingenious enough to invent yet other forms of warfare, and to use food, raw materials, finance, industrial power, ideology, and terrorism to subvert one another in an endless quest for supremacy and dominion. Nor can the present massive dislocation in the affairs of humanity be resolved through the settlement of specific conflicts or disagreements among nations. A genuine universal framework must be adopted. . . .

Racism, one of the most baneful and persistent evils, is a major barrier to peace. Its practice perpetrates too outrageous a violation of dignity of human beings to be countenanced under any pretext. Racism retards the unfoldment of the boundless potentialities of its victims, corrupts its perpetrators, and blights human progress. Recognition of the oneness of mankind, implemented by appropriate legal measures, must be universally upheld if this problem is to be overcome.

The inordinate disparity between rich and poor, a source of acute suffering, keeps the world in a state of instability, virtually on the brink of war. Few societies have dealt effectively with this situation. The solution calls for the combined application of spiritual, moral and practical approaches. A fresh look at the problem is required, entailing consultation with experts from a wide spectrum of disciplines, devoid of economic and ideological polemics, and involving the people directly affected in the decisions that must urgently be made. It is an issue that is bound up not only with the necessity for eliminating extremes of wealth and poverty but also with those spiritual verities the understanding of which can produce a new universal attitude. Fostering such an attitude is itself a major part of the solution.

Unbridled nationalism, as distinguised from a

sane and legitimate patriotism, must give way to a wider loyalty, to the love of humanity as a whole. Bahá'u'lláh's statement is: "The earth is but one country, and mankind its citizens." The concept of world citizenship is a direct result of the contraction of the world into a single neighborhood through scientific advances and of the indisputable interdependence of nations. Love of all the world's peoples does not exclude love of one's country. The advantage of the part in a world society is best served by promoting the advantage of the whole. Current international activities in various fields which nurture mutual affection and a sense of solidarity among peoples need greatly to be increased.

Religious strife, throughout history, has been the cause of innumerable wars and conflicts, a major blight to progress, and is increasingly abhorrent to the people of all faiths and no faith. Followers of all religions must be willing to face the basic questions which this strife raises, and to arrive at clear answers. How are the differences between them to be resolved, both in theory and in practice? The challenge facing the religious leaders of mankind is to contemplate, with hearts filled with the spirit of compassion and a desire for truth, the plight of humanity, and to ask themselves whether they cannot, in humility before their Almighty Creator, submerge their theological differences in a great spirit of mutual forbearance that will enable them to work together for the advancement of human understanding and peace.

The emancipation of women, the achievement of full equality between the sexes, is one of the most important, though less acknowledged prerequisites of peace. The denial of such equality perpetrates an injustice against one half of the world's population and promotes in men harmful attitudes and habits that are carried from the family to the workplace, to political life, and ultimately to international relations. There are no grounds, moral, practical, or biological, upon which such denial can be justified. Only as women are welcomed into full partnership in all fields of human endeavor will the moral and psychological climate be created in which international peace can emerge.

The cause of universal education, which has already enlisted in its service an army of dedicated people from every faith and nation, deserves the utmost support that the governments of the world can lend it. For ignorance is indisputably the principal reason for the decline and fall of peoples and the perpetuation of prejudice. No nation can achieve success unless education is accorded all its citizens. Lack of resources limits the ability of many nations to fulfil this necessity, imposing a certain ordering of priorities. The decision-making agencies involved would do well to consider giving first priority to the education of women and girls, since it is through educated mothers that the benefits of knowledge can be most effectively and rapidly diffused thoughout society. In keeping with the requirements of the times, consideration should also be given to teaching the concept of world citizenship as part of the standard education of every child.

A fundamental lack of communication between peoples seriously undermines efforts towards world peace. Adopting an international auxiliary language would go far to resolving this problem and necessitates the most urgent attention.

Two points bear emphasizing in all these issues. One is that the abolition of war is not simply a matter of signing treaties and protocols; it is a complex task requiring a new level of commitment to resolving issues not customarily associated with the pursuit of peace. Based on political agreements alone, the idea of collective security is a chimera. The other point is that the primary challenge in dealing with issues of peace is to raise the context to the level of principle, as distinct from pure pragmatism. For, in essence, peace stems from an inner state supported by a spiritual or moral attitude, and it is chiefly in evoking this attitude that the possibility of enduring solutions can be found.

THE UNIVERSAL HOUSE OF JUSTICE
Peace Statement, 1986

Integrity will give peace, justice will give lasting security. My people will live in a peaceful country.

JEWISH SCRIPTURES
The Prophet Isaiah

Womanly Times

Shall there be womanly times,
or shall we die?

IAN McEWAN
Or Shall We Die? 1983

Women are the bearers of
lifeloving energy. Ours is the task of deepening
that passion for life and separating from all that
threatens life, all that diminishes life; becoming
who we are as women; telling/living the truth of
our lives; shifting the weight of the world.

BARBARA ZANOTTI, 1982

Elise Boulding calls the . . .
arms race the "ultimate pathology of the twen-
tieth century." To do an effective plastic surgery

on this face . . . we need new images that offer creative alternatives to the centralized planning that runs us into the current batch of cul-de-sacs. These new images would be of futures calling forth a decentralist yet interconnected and inter-dependent world. In turn, such images depend on a "deeply spiritual faith that humankind is some-thing more, and human society meant to become something other than what we have realized so far in the human experience."

And who is likely to produce such images? People marginal to the present society, excluded from the centers of power, who see society with a fresh eye. . . .

The largest such marginal group, of course, is the world's women. Excluded from the going cor-ridors of power, they do not "belong" to the present system as men do. Utilizing the metaphor of the family, where they have domiciled, such women might stress the dimensions of mutuality and sharing that a successful family situation must have. In this stress they would be counter-ing the predominant male sense of the family, in which a strong father directs the lives of help-less children.

DENISE LARDNER CARMODY
Feminism and Christianity:
A Two Way Reflection, 1982

War will pass when intellectual culture and activity have made possible to the female an equal share in the governance of modern national life; it will probably not pass away much sooner; its extinction will not be delayed much longer.

It is especially in the domain of war that we, the bearers of men's bodies, who supply its most valuable munition, who, not amid the clamour and ardour of battle, but, singly, and alone, with a three-in-the-morning courage, shed our blood and face death that the battle-field may have its food, a food more precious to us than our heart's blood; it is we especially, who in the domain of war, have our word to say, a word no man can say for us. It is our intention to enter into the domain of war and to labour there till in the course of generations we have extinguished it.

OLIVE SCHREINER
Woman and Labour, 1911

The world of humanity is possessed of two wings: the male and the female. So long as these two wings are not equivalent in strength, the bird will not fly. Until womankind reaches the same degree as man, until she enjoys the same arena of activity, extraordinary attainment for humanity will not be realized; humanity cannot wing its way to heights of real attainment. When the two wings or parts become equivalent in strength, enjoying the same prerogatives, the flight of man will be exceedingly lofty and extraordinary. Therefore, woman must receive the same education as man and all inequality be adjusted. Thus, imbued with the same virtues as man, rising through all the degrees of human attainment, women will become the peers of men, and until this equality is established, true progress and attainment for the human race will not be facilitated.

The evident reasons underlying this are as follows: Woman by nature is opposed to war; she is an advocate of peace. Children are reared and brought up by the mothers who give them the first principles of education and labor assiduously in their behalf. Consider, for instance, a mother who has tenderly reared a son for twenty years to the age of maturity. Surely she will not consent to having that son torn asunder and killed in the field of battle. Therefore, as woman advances toward the degree of man in power and privilege, with the right of vote and control in human government, most assuredly war will cease; for woman is naturally the most devoted and staunch advocate of international peace.

'ABDU'L-BAHÁ
*The Promulgation
of Universal Peace,* 1912

The existence of nuclear weapons is killing us. Their production contaminates our environment, destroys our natural resources, and depletes our human energy and creativity. But the most critical danger they represent is to life itself. Sickness, accidents, genetic damage and death, these are the real products of the nuclear arms race. We say *no* to the threat of global holocaust, *no* to the arms race, *no* to death. We say *yes* to a world where people, animals, plants and the earth itself are respected and valued.

WOMEN'S ENCAMPMENT FOR A FUTURE
OF PEACE AND JUSTICE, 1983

Sisterhood is international—it does not stop at international borders. If we embrace militarism and conscription as part of equality we will be declaring our sisters as enemies. That is something we as women and as feminists will never do. We must refuse the mad rush toward military confrontation.

WOMEN'S INTERNATIONAL LEAGUE FOR
PEACE AND FREEDOM, 1980

It's very difficult for me to separate women and peace. By this I mean the following: as a man you can realize yourself in war. As far back as we know, men have realized themselves in war, there they have found their identity, their name (or epaulets to replace a name), their adventure, their life involvement—in short, themselves.

At the beginning of our culture stands a great epic which essentially deals with war, slaughter, military campaigns, conquest, looting, rape, duels, blood, death—the *Illiad*. Even the men who can't take part in this epic Trojan War have found in

it a cultural model for their identity. Human being equals man, and man equals hero—and this is
all realized in war, the great rite of passage.

Women's part in this great epic poem is peace,
the home, the farm, the olive trees. This means
that for their—very limited—self-realization,
women need peace.

A woman can't become a human being though,
with, or for war. You can become a "hyena of the
battlefield," like Brecht's Mother Courage; you
can imagine you're making a profit from war, but
you can't become a human being in this way. You
can only become a mother against war, not with
it, as Brecht convincingly portrayed: whenever
Courage strikes a bargain and tries to reorganize
herself economically through war, she loses one
of her children. These two roles—to be there for
war and to be there for the children—simply don't
go together. . . .

Given the presupposition of our culture, which
is a men's culture, nothing can change. Peace
needs other people, and other forms of behavior,
than those which have developed so far. Peace—if
we mean more by the word than the occasional
absence of war—needs women.

I don't mean that women are more peaceful or
better. I don't even know if their inhibitions
against killing are stronger than those of men. But

I do know that women are oppressed, that they are disadvantaged, exploited, raped—and that one of the means by which these things have happened and happen is war.

Women are not more peaceful, but they are more oppressed than are men. Therefore they are the natural allies of all who struggle against war and militarism. . . .

For women to become conscious of their situation means a break with the values with which we are raised, a break with the peacelessness with which we have been vaccinated. Militarism, use of violence, permanent preparation to exterminate others with a fist, is one of the central values of patriarchy. To become a woman means to become a woman for peace.

DOROTHEE SOLLE
"Peace Needs Women," 1983

Swords Into Plowshares

It shall come to pass in the latter days that the mountain of the house of the Lord shall be established as the highest of the mountains, and shall be raised above the hills; and all the nations shall flow to it, and many peoples shall come, and say: "Come, let us go up to the mountain of the Lord, to the house of the God of Jacob; that he may teach us his ways and that we may walk in his paths."

For out of Zion shall go forth the law, and the word of the Lord from Jerusalem. He shall judge between the nations, and shall decide for many peoples; and they shall beat their swords into plowshares, and their spears into pruning hooks; nation shall not lift up sword against nation, neither shall they learn war any more.

JEWISH SCRIPTURES
The Prophet Isaiah

I Deganawidah
and the chiefs of our Five Nations of the Great
    Peace
we now uproot the tallest pine
and beneath it we cast
all weapons of war

Deep into the earth
Into the underworld . . .
We cast all weapons of war.
We banish them from sight forever . . .
And replant the tree . . .
Thus shall the Great Peace be established.

NATIVE AMERICAN
Iroquois, Sixteenth Century

Come, behold the works of the Lord, . . .
He makes wars cease to the end of the earth;
    he breaks the bow, and shatters the spear,
    he burns the chariots with fire!
Be still, and know that I am God.

JEWISH SCRIPTURES
Psalms 46

Even ornamental weapons are not a source of happiness, but of dread. Therefore, the man of Tao will not abide where such things are. A good man at home sets the place of honor at his left hand. But the warrior, on going forth to battle, gives honor to the right hand. For weapons are things of ill omen. The man of enlightenment does not use them except when he cannot help it. His great desire is peace, and he does not take joy in conquest. To joy in conquest is to rejoice at the loss of human life. He who takes joy in bloodshed is not fit to govern the country.

TAOIST SCRIPTURES
Tao Te Ching

The people who walked in darkness have seen a great light; those who dwelt in a land of deep darkness, on them has light shined. Thou hast multiplied the nation, thou hast increased its joy; they rejoice before thee as with joy at the harvest, as men rejoice when they divide the spoil.

For the yoke of his burden, and the staff for his

shoulder, the rod of his oppressor, thou hast broken . . .

For every boot of the tramping warrior in battle tumult and every garment rolled in blood will be burned as fuel for the fire.

JEWISH SCRIPTURES
The Prophet Isaiah

O kings of the earth! Compose your differences and reduce your armaments, that the burden of your expenditures may be lightened, and that your minds and hearts may be tranquilized. Heal the dissensions that divide you, and ye will no longer be in need of any armaments except what the protection of your cities and territories demandeth. . . . We have learned that you are increasing your outlay every year, and are laying the burden . . . on your subjects. This, verily, is more than they can bear, and is a grievous injustice.

BAHÁ'I SCRIPTURES
Words of Bahá'u'lláh

Unused weapons are no less murderous—these require human energy and resources which are therefore not available to relieve desperate human needs. While a million dollars a minute is spent on the arms race, millions of people suffer malnutrition.

INTERNATIONAL FELLOWSHIP
OF RECONCILIATION

There is the well-known case of the ruler who is fostering peace and tranquility and at the same time devoting more energy than the warmongers to the accumulation of weapons and the building up of a larger army, on the grounds that peace and harmony can only be brought about by force. Peace is the pretext, and night and day they are all straining every nerve to pile up more weapons of war, and to pay for this their wretched people must sacrifice most of whatever they are able to earn by their sweat and toil. How many thousands have given up their work in useful industries and are laboring day and night to produce new and deadlier weapons which would spill out the blood of the race more copiously than before.

'ABDU'L-BAHÁ
The Secret of Divine Civilization, 1876

While so many people are going hungry, while so many families are suffering destitution, while so many people spend their lives submerged in the darkness of ignorance, while so many schools, hospitals, homes worthy of the name, are needed, every public or private squandering . . . every financially depleting arms race . . . all these we say become a scandalous and intolerable crime. The most serious obligation enjoined on us demands that we openly denounce it.

POPE PAUL VI

We are now living in the shadow of an arms race more intense, more costly, more widespread and more dangerous than the world has ever known. Never before has the human race been as close as it is now to total self-destruction. Today's arms race is an unparalleled waste of human and material resources; it threatens to turn the whole world into an armed camp; it aids repression and violates human rights; it promotes violence and insecurity in place of the security in whose name it is undertaken; it frustrates humanity's aspirations for justice and peace; it has no part in God's design for His world; it is demonic.

WORLD COUNCIL OF CHURCHES, 1978

We as concerned citizens recognize . . . that billions are being spent on arms, while people's basic needs, such as food, housing, health care, and education are underfunded; that to be able to kill and to be killed many times over in the name of defense is an evil waste of world resources.

UNITED CHURCH OF CHRIST, 1979

We cannot continue in this paralysing mistrust. If we want to work our way out of the desperate situation in which we find ourselves another spirit must enter into the people. It can only come if the awareness of its necessity suffices to give us strength to believe in its coming. We must presuppose the awareness of this need in all the peoples who have suffered along with us. We must approach them in the spirit that we are human beings, all of us, and that we feel ourselves fitted to feel with each other; to think and to will together in the same way.

The awareness that we are all human beings together has become lost in war and through politics. We have reached the point of regarding each other only as members of a people either allied with us or against us. Now we must rediscover the fact that we—all together—are human beings, and we must strive to concede to each other what moral capacity we have. Only in this way can we begin to believe that in other peoples as well as in ourselves there will arise the need for a new spirit which can be the beginning of a feeling of mutual trustworthiness toward each other.

At this stage we have the choice of two risks: the one lies in continuing the mad atomic arms race; . . . the other in the renunciation of nuclear weapons, and in the hope that America and the Soviet Union, and the peoples associated with them, will manage to live in peace. The first holds no hope of a prosperous future; the second does. We must risk the second.

ALBERT SCHWEITZER
Peace or Atomic War, 1958

By a general agreement all the governments of the world must disarm simultaneously . . . It will not do if one lays down the arms and the other refuses to do so. The nations of the world must concur with each other concerning this supremely important subject, thus they may abandon together the deadly weapons of human slaughter. As long as one nation increases her military and naval budget, another nation will be forced into this crazed competition through her natural and supposed interests . . .

Now the question of disarmament must be put into practice by all the nations and not only by one or two. Consequently the advocates of Peace must strive day and night, so that the individuals of every country may become peace-loving, public opinion may gain a strong and permanent footing, and day by day the army of International Peace be increased, complete disarmament be realized and the Flag of Universal Conciliation be waving on the summit of the mountains of the earth.

'ABDU'L-BAHÁ
"Questions and Answers," 1914

There has been no disarmament because the assumptions of the arms race have been almost universally accepted. Most people, including most people who favor disarmament, accept the premise that more weapons mean more security, that alternative systems of security not based on making hostages of hundreds of millions of people are utopian, and that the survival of the United States as a sovereign actor in the world justifies mass murder, poisoning of the earth, and the hideous mutation of the human species.

We do not seem to be able to generate the

moral passion to rid the world of arms because we ourselves are psychologically dependent upon them. The role of nuclear terrorism in our society is parallel to that of slavery a little over a hundred years ago. Like slavery, nuclear terrorism is a monstrous evil that mocks both our religious pretensions and our virtues. Both are dehumanizing. Both make victims of the innocent. Both are justified by worshiping power. Both support the comforts of the well-off and the aspiring. Both systems are addictive social drugs with a hold over society that cannot be broken except by the expression of extraordinary moral passion, courage, and the will to break free. The moderate use of nuclear weapons, like the moderate use of slavery, is impossible. . . . Systems have their own dynamics. Arms control—banning certain weapons while building others more efficient and more terrible—cannot succeed because it perpetuates, rather than challenges, the system of nuclear terrorism.

To say you are for disarmament means—unless you are indulging in official rhetoric—that you renounce the war system. Disarmament is a way of conveying intentions and establishing social commitments that are completely inconsistent with the use of blackmail, terror, and brute force as instruments of national policy. Most of us are unwilling to reflect on how much we depend upon the war system for personal security and comfort. That was also true of slavery, and for that reason more than two hundred years intervened between the first pangs of Quaker conscience and the Emancipation Proclamation.

As with slavery, our economic dependence upon the war system is profound as well as anachronistic. Both once made short-term economic sense; but the war system, like slavery, has outlasted its time because it blocks possibilities for much more efficient and rational use of resources and more effective means of developing power to solve political and social problems. . . .

At the dawn of the nuclear age Albert Einstein said that everything had changed but our thinking. When he said that politics was more difficult than physics he was emphasizing the extraordinary resistance we have to insights that could bring peace. Because thinking must fundamentally change if there is to be disarmament, and because fundamental change appears nearly impossible, the task of disarmament or ending the war system is more formidable than that of any social movement in history.

Recognizing this is necessary if we are to gather strength for the struggle. The peace movement has so little support, public opinion polls confirm, because of widespread feelings of power-lessness and universal mechanisms of denial. We feel powerless to alter the course of events, and so we deny both the danger and our responsibility to confront it.

But we will compound our feelings of power-lessness if we impose unreal expectations on ourselves. Many of us assume that once the facts are presented and the moral issues raised militaristic forces will disperse, so that we lose heart when they are not exorcised by a pamphlet or a march or a prayer. I believe that we need to see ourselves as part of a historic process, like the successive generations of abolitionists, to confront the institutions of war relentlessly and passionately, to build on the achievements of the peacemakers of the past, to honor our own achievements such as the ending of the Vietnam war, and to keep alive the faith that decency and rationality can prevail. Greater realism about the extraordinary obstacles to a security system based on disarmament can be inspiring rather than dispiriting because we can better understand both ourselves and the nature of the task.

A new security system for humankind is inevitable. The only question is whether it will come before nuclear war or after. More than any other issue, peace can command overwhelming majoritarian support. But disarmament, which is a mechanical technique for achieving peace, is not such an issue standing by itself. Zero nuclear weapons will be a reality on the day some clerk finds the last forgotten weapons in some abandoned warehouse and calls the department of waste disposal to get rid of them. To devalue them we need to delegitimize them, to keep stressing that whether or not they are exploded in anger, they cannot be used as instruments of power or as the foundation of security without destroying our society in the process.

RICHARD BARNET
"The Myth of Power,
The Power of Myth," 1978

One People, One World

After considerable difficulties, the man collects his powers and overcomes the obstacles to the unity of all men. Sadness gives way to joy.

CHINESE TRADITION
I Ching

Grant us peace, Thy most precious gift, O Thou eternal source of peace, and enable Israel to be its messenger unto the peoples of this earth. Strengthen the bonds of friendship and fellowship among the inhabitants of all lands. Plant virtue in every soul and may the love of Thy name hallow every heart. Praised be thou, O Lord, our God, giver of peace.

JEWISH TRADITION
Song of Peace

Whoever sees all beings in himself and himself in all beings does not, by virtue of such realization, hate anyone. . . . When, to that wise sage, all beings are realized as existing in his own self, then what illusion, what sorrow, can afflict him, perceiving as he does the Unity?

HINDU SCRIPTURE
Isa Upanishads

And other sheep I have, which are not of this fold: them also must I bring, and they shall hear my voice; and there shall be one fold, and one shepherd.

CHRISTIAN SCRIPTURES
The Gospel of John

All of God's creatures are His family. He is most beloved of God who does real good to the members of God's family.

ISLAMIC TRADITION
Words of Muhammad

The well-being of mankind, its peace and security, are unattainable unless and until its unity is firmly established.

BAHÁ'Í SCRIPTURES
Words of Bahá'u'lláh

If a man applies Tao to himself, his virtue will
  be genuine;
If he applies it to his family, his virtue will be
  abundant;
If he applies it to his village, his virtue will be
  lasting;

If he applies it to his nation, his virtue will be
    complete;
If he applies it to the world, his virtue will be
    universal.
Therefore, by his person he may observe
    persons;
    by his family he may observe families;
    by his village he may observe villages;
    by his country he may observe countries;
And by his world he may observe worlds.

TAOIST SCRIPTURES
Tao Te Ching

In cycles gone by, though har-
mony was established, yet, owing to the absence
of means, the unity of all mankind could not
have been achieved. Continents remained widely
divided, nay even among the peoples of one and
the same continent association and interchange of
thought were well nigh impossible. Consequently
intercourse, understanding and unity amongst all
the peoples and kindreds of the earth were unattainable. In this day, however, means of commu-

nication have multiplied, and the five continents of the earth have virtually merged into one. . . . In like manner all the members of the human family, whether peoples or governments, cities or villages, have become increasingly interdependent. For none is self-sufficiency any longer possible, inasmuch as political ties unite all peoples and nations, and the bonds of trade and industry, of agriculture and education, are being strengthened every day. Hence the unity of all mankind can in this day be achieved. Verily this is none other but one of the wonders of this wondrous age, this glorious century. Of this past ages have light—has been endowed with unique and unprecedented glory, power and illumination. Hence the miraculous unfolding of a fresh marvel every day. miraculous unfolding of a fresh marvel every day. Eventually it will be seen how bright its candles will burn in the assemblage of man.

Behold how its light is now dawning upon the world's darkened horizon. The first candle is unity in the political realm, the early glimmerings of which can now be discerned. The second candle is unity of thought in world undertakings, the consummation of which will ere long be witnessed. The third candle is unity in freedom which will surely come to pass. The fourth candle is unity in religion which is the corner-stone of the foundation itself, and which, by the power of God, will be revealed in all its splendor. The fifth candle is the unity of nations—a unity which in this century will be securely established, causing all the peoples of the world to regard themselves as citizens of one common fatherland. The sixth candle is unity of races, making of all that dwell on earth peoples and kindreds of one race. The seventh candle is unity of language, i.e., the choice of a universal tongue in which all peoples will be instructed and converse. Each and every one of these will inevitably come to pass, inasmuch as the power of the Kingdom of God will aid and assist in their realization.

'ABDU'L-BAHÁ
"Seven Candles of Unity"

We are one, after all, you and I; together we suffer, together exist, and forever will recreate each other.

PIERRE TEILHARD DE CHARDIN (1881–1955)

In the closed sphere of the exclusively political, there is no way to penetrate to the factual of men nor to relieve the existential mistrust which divides the world into hostile camps . . . whose "natural end" is the technically perfect suicide of the entire human race. The solidarity of all separate groups in the flaming battle for the becoming of one humanity is, in the present hour, the highest duty on earth. . . . In every decision we must struggle, with fear and trembling, lest it burden us with greater guilt than we are compelled to assume, with dangerous arrogance, too, if we believed that any individual, any nation, any ideology, has a monopoly on rightness, liberty, and human dignity.

MARTIN BUBER (1878–1965)

The split in today's world is perceptible even to a hasty glance. Any of our contemporaries readily identifies two world powers, each of them already capable of utterly destroying the other. However, the understanding of the split too often is limited to this political conception: the illusion according to which danger may be abolished through successful diplomatic negotiations or by achieving a balance of armed forces. The truth is that the split is both more profound and more alienating, that the rifts are more numerous than one can see at first glance. These deep manifold splits bear the danger of equally manifold disaster for all of us, in accordance with the ancient truth that a kingdom—in this case, our Earth—divided against itself cannot stand.

ALEXANDER SOLZHENITSYN
A World Split Apart, 1979

Among all the things ordained for our happiness, the greatest is universal peace . . . To achieve this state of universal good, a single world government is necessary.

DANTE
De Monarchia, Thirteenth Century

Collective security without collective sovereignty is meaningless ... Only a legal order can bring security.

EMERY REEVES
The Anatomy of Peace, 1945

The popes of the last seven decades have never tired of calling for a world order of peace. Today, we know more than ever how important it is to have a world order of peace. In a world where everything and everybody is interrelated on a hitherto unknown scale, it has become an urgent ethical commandment. The international organizations have "been the object of attempts at manipulation on the part of nations wishing to exploit such bodies" in the course of the last few centuries (John Paul II). This must not lead to discouragement and resignation. Instead, we must give fresh thought to the individual structures of the international organization in order to take into account the new realities and conflicts. Every chance must be seized in order to "regain for the organizations the mission which is theirs by virtue of their origin, their charter and their mandate." . . .

The Second Vatican Council put forward the proposal that "a universally recognized world authority should be established, possessing adequate power and authority to assure the protection and safety of all, guaranteeing justice and the observation of human rights". Pope Paul VI submitted this proposal in his historic address before the plenary session of the United Nations on October 4, 1965. Such a world authority designed to protect freedom and peace must not be created along the lines of a centralist unitary state. The principle of giving help to those who practice self-help forms the necessary adjunct to the principle of solidarity among all nations. By the same token, the states must be prepared to surrender part of their sovereignty. In order to apply international law we must above all establish a world court of justice whose decisions shall be binding and which will be accompanied by the requisite power of imposing sanctions. Such proposals may appear utopian against the background of the political reality of our times. In the long run, however, there is no alternative way of creating the foundations for a dignified, free and fair coexistence between all nations. Until this goal has been achieved, we must continue to seek interim solutions for safeguarding peace.

JOINT PASTORAL LETTER OF
THE GERMAN BISHOPS, 1984

If we are serious about nuclear disarmament—the minimum technical requirement for real safety from extinction—then we must accept conventional disarmament as well, and this means disarmament not just of nuclear powers but of all powers, for the present nuclear powers are hardly likely to throw away their conventional arms while non-nuclear powers hold on to theirs. But if we accept both nuclear and conventional disarmament, then we are speaking of revolutionizing the politics of the earth . . . We must lay down our arms, relinquish sovereignty, and found a political system for the peaceful settlement of international disputes.

JONATHAN SCHELL
The Fate of the Earth, 1982

If the name of the country has such a nature as to create bonds between those who have a common country, why do not men resolve then that the earth should become the country of all?

ERASMUS
Peace Protests, Sixteenth Century

Apart from an effective inspection system to supervise the disarmament process from the outset, it will be indispensable simultaneously to establish an adequate world police force in order that, after complete disarmament has been accomplished, the means will exist to deter or apprehend violators of the world law forbidding any national armaments and prohibiting violence or the threat of it between nations. It will then become equally clear that along with the prohibition of violence or the threat of it as the means of dealing with international disputes, it will be essential to establish alternative peaceful means to deal with all disputes between nations in the shape of a world judicial and conciliation system. It will doubtless also be found advisable, in the interest of a solid and durable peace, to include a World Development Authority, adequately and reliably financed, in order to mitigate the vast disparities between the "have" and the "have not" nations.

The necessity will also be seen for a world legislature with carefully limited yet adequate powers. . . . In addition, it will be necessary to constitute an effective world executive, free from any crippling veto, in order to direct and control the world inspection service and the world police force and to exercise other essential executive functions. Finally, it will follow as surely as day follows night that an effective world revenue system must be adopted.

GRENVILLE CLARK AND LOUIS B. SOHN
World Peace Through World Law, 1960

Some form of a world Super-State must needs be evolved, in whose favor all the nations of the world will have willingly ceded every claim to make war, certain rights to impose taxation and all rights to maintain armaments, except for purposes of maintaining internal order within their respective dominions. Such a state will have to include within its orbit an International Executive adequate to enforce supreme and unchallengeable authority on every recalcitrant member of the commonwealth; a World Parliament whose members shall be elected by the people in their respective countries and whose election shall be confirmed by their respective governments; and a Supreme Tribunal whose judgment will have a binding effect even in such cases where the parties concerned did not voluntarily agree to submit their case to its consideration. A world community in which all economic barriers will have permanently demolished and the interdependence of Capital and Labor definitely recognized; in which the clamor of religious fanaticism and strife will have been forever stilled; in which the flame of racial animosity will have been finally extinguished; in which a single code of international law—the product of the considered judgment of the world's federated representatives—shall have as its sanction the instant and coercive intervention of the combined forces of the federated units; and finally a world community in which the fury of a capricious and militant nationalism will have been transmuted into

an abiding consciousness of world citizenship—
such indeed, appears, in its broadest outline, the
Order anticipated by Bahá'u'lláh, an Order that
shall come to be regarded as the fairest fruit of
a slowly maturing age.

SHOGHI EFFENDI
"The Goal of a New World Order," 1931

Today, while "experts" calmly
discuss the possibility of the United States being
able to survive a war if *"only fifty million"* (!) of
the population are killed, when the Chinese speak
of being able to *spare* "three hundred million" and
"still get along," it is obvious that we are no
longer in the realm where moral truth is conceiv-
able. The only sane course that remains is to
work frankly and without compromise for a
supranational authority and for the total abolition of war.

THOMAS MERTON
"Peace: A Religious Responsibility," 1962

The time has arrived when religions, instead of antagonizing each other because of what we once thought were religious convictions, should cooperate with each other in order to contribute to the cause of mankind and world peace, because, in the final analysis, all sectors of religion are bound together by the common aspiration for human happiness and salvation. This must be . . . the responsibility of us religionists who are called upon to realize on earth the will of God and the spirit of Buddha. . . . We Buddhists practice the Way, aiming to achieve spiritual peace and enlightenment, and establish the Land of Serene Light. When we are asked what this peaceful place, the Land of Serene Light, is, we . . . explain by saying that we would use a world federation, a world state, as our blueprint.

NIKKYŌ NIWANO
A Buddhist Approach to Peace, 1977

Nuclear holocaust is five minutes away. But maybe those minutes are the graced moments in which God is speaking to all of humanity. We have no option but to go the way of peace. Maybe God is using this threat to give us the opportunity to recognize our common humanity, to bring us into the one world, the one community, the one family of God.

BISHOP WALTER SULLIVAN, 1982

It is incumbent upon every man of insight and understanding to strive to translate that which hath been written into reality and action. . . . That one indeed is a man who, today, dedicateth himself to the service of the entire human race. . . . It is not for him to pride himself who loveth his own country, but rather for him who loveth the whole world. The earth is but one country, and mankind its citizens.

BAHÁ'Í SCRIPTURES
Words of Bahá'u'lláh

117